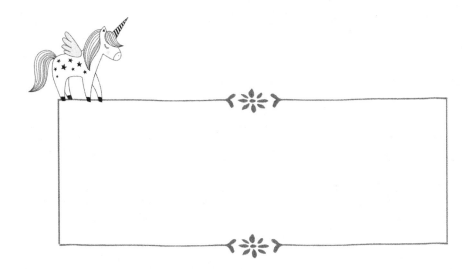

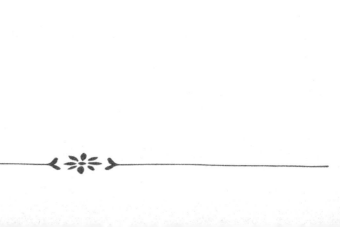

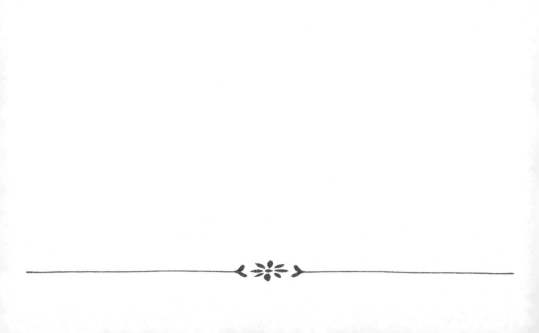

Love all, trust a few, do wrong to none.

— Shakespeare

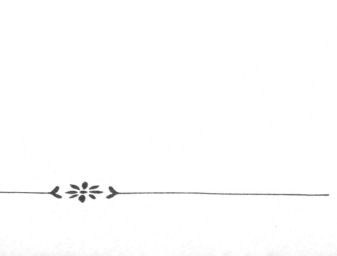

This above all: to thine ownself be true.

– Shakespeare

_____

_____

_____

_____

_____

_____

_____

_____

_____

_____

_____

_____

_____

_____

_____

_____

_____

_____

_____

_____

_____

_____

Excellence is not an act, but a habit.

– Aristotle

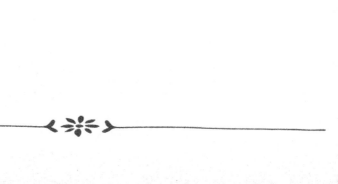

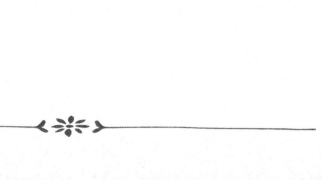

No act of kindness, no matter how small, is
ever wasted.
— Aesop

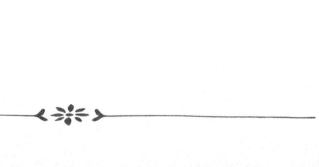

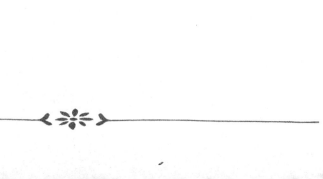

The way to be happy is to make others so.

– Robert Ingersoll

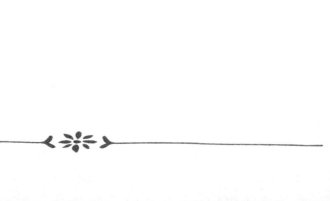

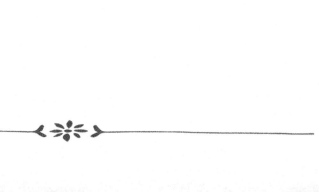

She is clothed in strength and
dignity and she laughs without fear
of the future.

— Proverbs 31:25 KJV

Peace is always beautiful.

– Walt Whitman

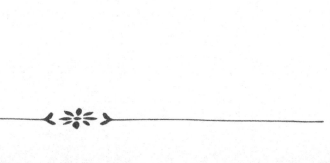

_____

_____

_____

_____

_____

_____

_____

_____

_____

_____

_____

_____

_____

_____

_____

_____

_____

_____

_____

_____

_____

I am not bothered by the fact that I am
not understood.

— Confucius

Bloom where you are planted.

- 1 Corinthians KJV

Made in the USA
Middletown, DE
15 February 2019